U.S.-China Economic and Security Review Commission
Staff Research Backgrounder

June 9, 2014

The China-Russia Gas Deal:
Background and Implications for the Broader Relationship

by

Iacob Koch-Weser
Policy Analyst, Economics and Trade

with

Craig Murray
Senior Analyst, Security and Foreign Affairs

Contents

Introduction

During President Vladimir Putin's state visit to Beijing on May 21, China and Russia signed a 30-year gas supply agreement worth $400 billion. By 2020, Russia intends to export 38 billion cubic meters (bcm) of gas to China each year from untapped fields in East Siberia. To be implemented, the deal could require $80 billion worth of new production and pipeline infrastructure.[i] President Putin claims that this will be the "largest construction project in the world over the next four years."[1] The deal is notable not only for its size and duration but for its timing. Ten years of negotiations were finally concluded at a sensitive juncture for Russia, as it faces the threat of tougher sanctions over its handling of the Ukraine crisis.

The deal has prompted divergent reactions. Some argue that China cut a good deal;[ii] others contend that it is incurring unnecessary risks.[2] Some assert that the deal is purely about energy, prefaced by detailed negotiations between Russia's Gazprom and China's oil major China National Petroleum Corporation (CNPC);[3] others point to geopolitical calculations.[iii] Some analysts counsel us to "ignore the hype,"[4] given the deal's challenging and slow implementation; others see "significant implications for relations between Beijing and Moscow, the European energy market, energy security in the Asia-Pacific, and even the pace of climate change."[5]

Drawing on existing policy literature[iv] and additional data, this paper examines the Sino-Russian gas deal, with a focus on China. It aims to clarify the conditions, motives, and implications of the deal. Its general conclusions are that:

- *Preconditions have been in place for years, but central points of contention took time to resolve.* China is keen to raise the share of gas in its energy mix and to improve its bargaining leverage in the global gas market. Gazprom seeks to diversify toward Asia to reduce its reliance on Europe, explore new reserves in the Far East, and retake market share from liquefied natural gas (LNG) producers. The decade-long gas contract talks have been improving for the past three to four years, culminating in a memorandum of understanding (MOU) in March 2013 that resolved issues of shipping routes and volume. Still, an agreement did not materialize until now due to disagreement on price, payment, and investment conditions.

- *China may look the immediate winner in the gas deal but may not have bargained hard enough.* On several fronts, China seems to benefit more than Russia. The price of the gas shipments, long the stumbling block in the negotiations, remains an official secret, but consensus estimates are that it was lowered in China's favor. Russia has agreed to ship the gas via the Eastern route,

---

[i] This estimate is based on the sum of Gazprom's estimated investment of $55 billion, and China's reported pre-payment of $25 billion. Paul J. Saunders, "The Not-So-Mighty Russia-China Gas Deal," *The National Interest*, May 23, 2014. *http://nationalinterest.org/feature/the-not-so-mighty-russia-china-gas-deal-10518?page=2.*

[ii] A proponent of this view is Gordon Kwan, head of oil and gas research at Nomura International Hong Kong Ltd. See Aibing Guo, "PetroChina, Utilities Stand to Gain from Russia Gas Deal," Bloomberg, May 22, 2014, via Factiva.

[iii] Shamil Yenikeyeff, a research fellow at the Oxford Institute for Energy Studies, states that "Russia needs this China deal very badly because it needs to signal to [Brussels] and to some EU nations that it is taking a step that is economically profitable and that it's found a new market for its gas." Quoted in Vanessa Mock, "Russia Racing to Clinch Energy Deal With China; Moscow Needs to Show its Major Customer Europe It Has New Market for Its Gas, Says Researcher," *Wall Street Journal*, May 21, 2014, via Factiva.

[iv] For recent studies on Sino-Russian relations in the gas sector, see Andrew C. Kuchins, "Russia and CIS in 2013: Russia's Pivot to Asia," *Asian Survey* 54:1 (January/February 2014): 129-137; Elena Shadrina and Michael Bradshaw, "Russia's Energy Governance Transitions and Implications for Enhanced Cooperation with China, Japan, and South Korea," *Post-Soviet Affairs* 29:6 (2013): 461-499; Keun-Wook Paik, "Through the Dragon Gate? A Window of Opportunity for Northeast Asian Gas Security" (London, UK: Chatham House, May 2012); Keun-Wook Paik, "The Role of Russian Gas in China's Energy Supply Strategy." *Asia Europe Journal* 11:3 (2013): 323-338; Morena Skalamera, "Booming Synergies in Sino-Russian Natural Gas Partnership" (Cambridge, MA: Harvard Kennedy School, Belfer Center for Science and International Affairs, May 2014); Morena Skalamera, "Pipeline Pivot: Why Russia and China Are Poised to Make Energy History" (Cambridge, MA: Harvard Kennedy School, Belfer Center for Science and International Affairs, May 2014); Paul J. Saunders, "The Not-So-Mighty Russia-China Gas Deal," *The National Interest*, May 23, 2014. *http://nationalinterest.org/feature/the-not-so-mighty-russia-china-gas-deal-10518?page=2.*

reducing Gazprom's arbitrage opportunities between Europe and China. Moreover, CNPC incurs less upfront investment risk than Gazprom. Even so, China is incurring other risks, including a failure to secure equity investment in the Siberian gas fields; the potential for Russia to index the price to oil; Russia's potential inability to deliver enough gas; and an impending supply glut in the gas industry that could render the negotiated price too high. Given Russia's difficult position and asymmetries between the two parties, China perhaps could have pushed a harder bargain.

- *Long-term energy interests laid the foundation, but broader bilateral interests secured the deal.* Broader interests in the energy, economic, and security realm likely helped push the deal over the finish line. A legacy of mistrust and strategic confrontation still affects the Sino-Russian relationship. But since 2012, well before the Ukraine crisis, Sino-Russian ties have been warming in the form of frequent state visits, broader and deeper military relations, and coordinated United Nations Security Council (UNSC) voting on Syria and the Crimea. During President Putin's May visit, the two presidents' statements hewed closely on diverse strategic issues; concurrently, over 30 commercial deals were signed, several of which are of a long-term strategic nature.

- *Beijing is pursuing broader security and economic interests.* The gas deal is likely part of Beijing's broader effort to advance security cooperation with Moscow, while countering U.S. power and influence in Central and East Asia. These objectives have received greater priority under President Xi Jinping. Further, the $400 billion gas deal was only one of several bilateral energy agreements, which taken together constitute an elevation from crude oil trade to petrochemical processing and gas shipments. Closer economic cooperation with Russia also benefits a range of non-energy interest groups in China, spanning manufacturing, logistics, and finance.

- *The deal's impact on gas consumers and producers is nuanced and will take time to discern.* The deal could diversify existing supplies and lower the price of gas, but this effect is not universally beneficial to the United States and its allies. For gas producers, the prospect of more pipeline gas could disincentivize investment in the liquefied natural gas sector, potentially affecting LNG production in the United States and the build-out of LNG ports. Under certain long-run scenarios, the deal could also negatively impact Japanese and European access to Russian gas.

- *The deal could mitigate the impact of U.S. and European sanctions on Russia.* The deal is unlikely to change the dynamic of the Ukraine crisis, as Russia will continue to depend on European gas consumers. Still, the $400 billion contract with China may mitigate the impact of Western economic sanctions. Further, it gives positive publicity to Russian energy elites targeted by Washington and Brussels.

1. Setting Up the Deal: Preconditions and Points of Contention

Preconditions for the Deal

(1) Long-term Trends in the Gas Market and China's Energy Needs

Industry experts have expected China and Russia to sign a gas supply deal for several years now. Morena Skalamera, a scholar at the Harvard Kennedy School's "Geopolitics of Energy Project," published a paper just prior to the May summit, which accurately predicted that "Russia and China are poised to make energy history."[6] Several factors have laid the groundwork. The first relates to long-term trends in the gas sector and China's energy needs. Natural gas has been the world's most dynamic energy source over the past decade. Technological innovations, led by gas liquefaction and storage and unconventional gas recovery, have made the resource more price-competitive, abundant, and tradable. Gas is also cleaner than coal and petroleum, rendering it attractive to policymakers concerned about climate change and air pollution. Other clean alternatives, like nuclear, hydro, and wind power, tend to have problems in terms of safety, feasibility, or cost competitiveness.

Natural gas use in China is still at an early stage. At present, it only comprises 5 percent of China's energy mix, and will take many decades to replace coal, which accounts for nearly 70 percent. In the oil sector, China has overtaken the United States as the world's largest importer and consumer. By contrast, China ranks fourth among the world's gas consumers, and in 2012, imported less gas than neighboring Japan and South Korea (see Appendix Tables A-1 and A-2.2). Imports now make up roughly one-third of China's gas consumption, versus over half of its oil consumption (see Figure 1).

Figure 1: China's Production and Consumption of Natural Gas through 2012
(billions cubic meters; rate %)

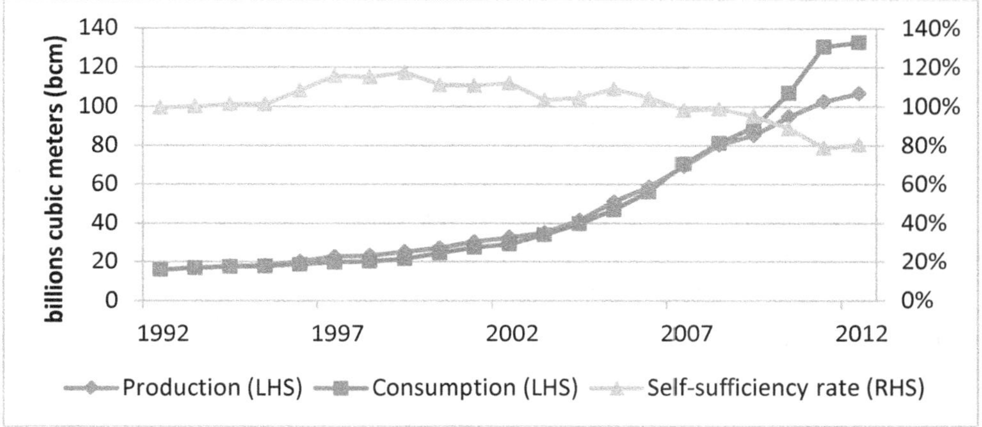

Source: China National Bureau of Statistics, via CEIC data.
Note: Precise figures on China's gas import reliance vary. According to the CNPC Economics and Technology Research Institute, China's natural gas external dependence in 2013 was 31.6 percent. [7]

Nonetheless, China's gas consumption is growing rapidly, with strong policy support from Beijing. China's energy planners expect gas to account for 12 percent of China's national energy mix by 2030.[8] It is still not as cheap as coal, but the price gap is narrowing, driven in part by government-enforced price controls. An immediate incentive is to reduce the severe air pollution in China's urban centers. About 70 percent of the country's total energy is consumed by industry.[v] The government is seeking to shed excess capacity and raise efficiencies, yet diversifying into cleaner energy sources such as gas may be more amenable to policymakers who are looking to sustain industrial output. Meanwhile, China's efforts to develop clean coal facilities, connect wind and solar power to the grid, and build nuclear reactors will take at least a decade to make a substantial impact on energy use.

China's rate of gas imports and consumption is outpacing that of other countries, a trend likely to continue given the country's vast energy needs (see Appendix Table A-2.2). The consultancy Wood Mackenzie projects China's gas consumption needs to quadruple in the next 20 years (see Table 1).[9] How this will impact imports is debatable – experts disagree about how much China will be able to produce domestically. According to the International Energy Agency, China will need to import 40 percent of its gas use by 2035, while Wood Mackenzie's forecast implies only 17 percent import reliance by 2030.[10] Either way, China is likely to be the main driver of global gas imports in the next two decades.

---

[v] This number is based on 2012 data from China National Bureau of Statistics, via CEIC data.

Table 1: Projection of China's Future Production and Consumption of Gas (Wood Mackenzie)

	Production (bcm)	Consumption (bcm)	Implied imports (bcm)	Import ratio (%)
2000	26.6	24.5	2.0	0.0%
2011	101.2	128.8	-27.6	21.4%
2030	449.7	541.7	-92.0	17.0%

Source: Adapted from Bill White, "Stakes Are Big in Russia-China Gas Supply Talks" (Alaska Natural Gas Transportation Projects: Office of the Regional Coordinator, February 11, 2013.)

(2) China's Gas Import Strategy

A second factor driving the gas deal is China's need to optimize its gas imports. In the mid-2000s, China was able to sign long-term off-take agreements[vi] with the world's largest LNG exporter, Qatar. With the completion of the first and second West-East Pipeline in 2009-2011, China has also been able to import Central Asian gas into China at very low prices. More recently, however, the global gas boom has made suppliers more reluctant to sign long-term off-take agreements, forcing China to source more gas through traders in the LNG spot market. Because the gas industry is not nearly as globally integrated as the oil market, there is little opportunity for arbitrage; Asian spot market rates are currently much higher than gas prices in the United States and Europe. For China, the result is a higher cost of imports (see Figure 2).

Meanwhile, China's three national oil companies (NOCs), which source the majority of China's gas imports, are subject to strict price controls in the domestic market. To subsidize domestic heating and electricity use, the National Development and Reform Commission (NDRC) effectively restricts the NOCs from passing on higher import prices to consumers. PetroChina, CNPC's subsidiary, claims to have lost billions on imports of LNG and pipeline gas.[11]

Figure 2: Volume and Price per Unit of China's LNG Imports
(tons millions; $ / ton)

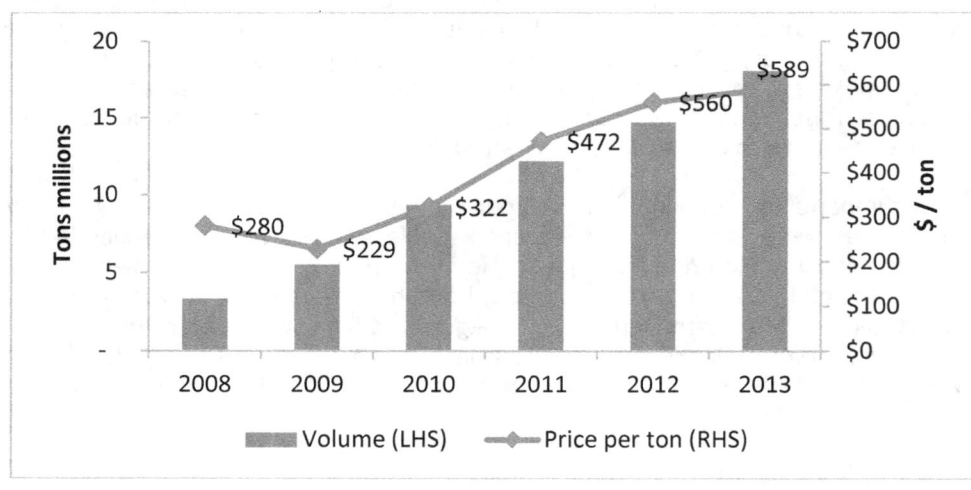

Source: China General Administration of Customs, via CEIC data.

[vi] An off-take agreement is an agreement between a producer of a resource and a buyer of a resource to purchase/sell portions of the producer's future production. It is normally negotiated prior to the construction of a facility (e.g., a gas field and related infrastructure) to secure a market for the future output of the facility. If lenders can see the company will have a purchaser of its production, it is easier to obtain financing. Definition from Investopedia. *http://www.investopedia.com/terms/o/offtake-agreement.asp.*

Faced with a price squeeze, China's NOCs can ill afford to spend more per unit of imports. China may consider any of three primary ways to overcome this dilemma. One, of course, is to raise the domestic price of gas. The NDRC has experimented with reforms to liberalize wellhead prices for shale gas and has launched a pilot scheme to link domestic natural gas pricing to imported fuels in Guangdong and Guangxi. [12] Last July, a year-and-a-half after conducting these plot tests, the government enacted a market-oriented gas pricing mechanism, along with a 15 percent increase in the government-set wholesale price for non-residential users. [13] However, the NDRC is reluctant to pass on the full cost of imported gas, given the impact this could have on industrial output and consumer inflation. Poorer provinces in the interior are particularly vulnerable to price hikes. [14]

Another option is to increase domestic gas production. China in 2012 ranked just seventh in global gas production, with about 3 percent of global output. [15] But China's gas reserves, when factoring in unconventional gas, rival those of Russia and the United States. Researchers from CNPC predict domestic production to increase dramatically by 2030. China's NOCs are trying to expedite this process by inviting foreign companies into production partnerships and investing in shale gas exploration in North America. [vii] Some early gains have been made, particularly in Sichuan province. Skeptics, however, do not see much future potential, given China's suboptimal geology, water scarcity, and institutional constraints (e.g., limits on foreign investment and unfair bidding processes for new fields).

Increasing China's gas pipeline imports thus becomes a pragmatic choice. If imported in sufficient volumes, pipelined gas can increase China's bargaining leverage vis-à-vis the LNG market, both directly in negotiations with suppliers, and indirectly by lowering the LNG spot price. For many Chinese analysts and policymakers, pipeline imports also help to mitigate China's "Malacca dilemma," or perceived vulnerability to potential efforts by other countries (such as the United States) to blockade Chinese energy imports at maritime chokepoints. Related to this is China's concern about sourcing energy from the Middle East, given that region's political instability (Arab Spring, Iran, Syria). In this context, Eurasian countries are attractive partners: their proven gas reserves are comparable to the Middle East (see Appendix Table A-3), and land-based supply routes beyond Central Asia are limited. [viii]

An abiding belief in the "safety" of land-based transport may be misguided, given that pipelines are also liable to attack and disruption. [16] It is important to distinguish, however, between oil and gas. Maritime imports will continue to make up the vast majority of China's oil imports, the bulk of which is sourced from the Middle East and Africa. In contrast, pipeline gas accounted for 46 percent of China's gas imports in 2011. This is the result of the West-East pipeline that began to ferry gas from Turkmenistan, Uzbekistan, and Kazakhstan to China in 2009. [17] China is eager to build on the initial success of the West-East Pipeline project, both by extending this network within China and by building new transnational pipeline infrastructure in the northeast of the country. [18]

[vii] In China, Sinopec has signed agreements over the past five years with ConocoPhillips, Chevron, and Total to explore shale in Jiangsu, Anhui, Guizhou, and Sichuan provinces. The Italian gas giant Eni also agreed in March of last year to partner with CNPC to develop the 2,000 square-km Rongchang block in Sichuan province. In the United States, Sinopec agreed in 2012 to buy $2.5 billion worth of shale-gas assets in Ohio, Michigan, and other areas from Devon Energy Corp. That followed CNOOC's $2.2 billion purchase in 2010 of assets owned by Oklahoma-based Chesapeake Energy Corp. and a smaller acquisition in 2011. Lianna Brirded, "Shale Gas: International Firms Tap Into China's Lucrative Market," *International Business Times*, May 17, 2013, via Factiva; Joseph Boris, "Resourceful Thinking," *China Daily*, February 8, 2013, via Factiva.

[viii] China is mulling other gas import projects: (1) a $2.3 billion China-Burma pipeline; (2) an Asian version of the Panama Canal in Southern Thailand, which has yet to materialize after a decade of talks; (3) an extension of the West-East Pipeline through Turkmenistan to source gas from Iran; and (4) a Xinjiang-Gwadar development corridor with long-term ally Pakistan, which entails building a port at Gwadar in the province of Balochistan to get direct access to oil and gas from the Middle East and North Africa. Related to this, China has recently invested $4.2 billion to develop gas in Mozambique. Loro Horta, "The Dragon Looks West: China and Central Asia," *IPRIS Viewpoints* (October 2013), pp.1-3.

(3) Russia's "Asia Pivot"

Another important precondition for the Sino-Russian gas deal is Moscow's "Asia pivot," shorthand for stronger commercial ties with Russia's eastern neighbors. So far, Asia's role in Russia's gas shipments has been limited. Russia began to export gas to Asia around 2009 but last year still sent merely 7 percent of its exports there (see Table 2). The gas projects that Russia is pursuing in East Siberia and the Far East are primarily on Sakhalin Island, off the Pacific coast, where Russian firms Gazprom and Rosneft are partnering with Western energy companies (see Appendix Table A-4). In 2009, however, Moscow unveiled its "Energy Strategy 2030," which envisions a fundamental reform of the country's energy sector to become more efficient, profitable, and sustainable. The Strategy prioritizes development of new oil and gas deposits in East Siberia and the Far East, in tandem with more gas sales to Asia. [19]

While the booming Asian market is a "pull" factor, [20] it is hard to ignore the "push" factors behind the "Asia pivot." Russia's economy has been plagued by slow growth, high debt and inflation, and declining investor confidence since the global financial crisis. Oil and gas exports account for 52 percent of Russia's government budget, which has fallen into deficit in the last two years. [21][ix] Balancing the books is now premised on ever higher oil prices and on heavy taxation of the country's energy firms. Firms like Gazprom have lacked the capital to invest in new gas fields, particularly in the resource-rich Far East. Nadym-pur-Taz, the gas field that accounts for 90 percent of total Russian gas production, has already peaked. [22] According to one estimate by a Russian think tank, Russia will need to invest $700 billion until 2030 just to keep physical volumes of production in its energy sector at current levels. [23]

Table 2: Russia's Natural Gas Exports by Region

Volume (bcm)

	2008	2009	2010	2011	2012	2013 (est.)
EU-28	124.6	104.8	107.6	110.4	104.8	124.6
Non-EU and Turkey	31.1	22.7	19.8	25.5	22.7	25.5
CIS	70.8	48.1	59.5	59.5	56.6	45.3
Asia	--	5.7	14.2	14.2	14.2	14.2
TOTAL	226.5	181.2	201.1	209.5	198.2	209.5

Share (%)

	2008	2009	2010	2011	2012	2013 (est.)
EU-28	55.0%	57.8%	53.5%	52.7%	52.9%	59.5%
Non-EU and Turkey	13.8%	12.5%	9.9%	12.2%	11.4%	12.2%
CIS	31.3%	26.6%	29.6%	28.4%	28.6%	21.6%
Asia	0.0%	3.1%	7.0%	6.8%	7.1%	6.8%
TOTAL	100.0%	100.0%	100.0%	100.0%	100.0%	100.0%

Source: Adapted from Sergey Paltsev, "Scenarios for Russia's Natural Gas Exports to 2050," *Energy Economics* 42 (2014): 265.

Russia's preeminence in the global gas market is also waning. According to 2012 numbers, Russia (20.1 percent share) remains the world's top gas exporter, with Qatar (11.6 percent) ranking a distant second (see Appendix Table A-2.1). But market share is being eroded by the shale revolution in the United States and LNG exports from the Middle East and Asia-Pacific. A decade ago, experts warned of a potential shortage of Russian gas exports, as European demand outstripped Russian supply; today, increases in global supply have prompted predictions of surplus Russian gas. [24] The United States has surpassed

---

[ix] For Russia, overreliance on oil and gas exports presents structural risks, such as "Dutch disease," a scenario in which a resource windfall causes an influx of dollars, making local currency scarce. When dollars are converted, the local currency appreciates in value. The result is that goods exports become more expensive, putting the export sector out of work (which can only be offset by less labor-intensive resource sector jobs). Influx of dollars also increases domestic demand as cash is more freely available, and that can lead to inflation. If spent on domestic goods, excess demand can also push up prices of other resources that are in limited supply, such as labor, which tends to hurt manufacturers.

Russia as the world's largest gas producer on account of shale production – Russia is rumored to have abandoned Arctic gas fields at Shtokman due to a reduction in U.S. demand. While new shale gas reserves are being discovered around the world, Russia ranks only ninth in technically recoverable shale reserves.[25]

Gazprom, Russia's top gas producer, earns the bulk of its revenue by pipelining gas at a premium to Western Europe (see Table 3). Due to reduced U.S. demand for gas imports, more gas (as well as U.S. coal) supply has become available for the European market. Gazprom, still Europe's top supplier, is now losing market share there (32 percent in 2010 to 26 percent in 2012). Several European clients have also begun revising their long-term contracts with the Russian company. Gazprom has converted 15 percent of contractual volumes in Europe to lower spot prices; reduced its take-or-pay provision – the amount customers are forced to pay, regardless of actual consumption – from 85 percent to 60 percent; and paid an estimated $4 billion in refunds to European customers in 2012-2013.[26]

In a next phase, European actions against Russia could become more aggressive. The European Commission is alleging that Gazprom's extensive control of both gas production and supply in Central and Eastern Europe breaches EU competition rules. Litigation has been suspended for the time-being but could be resumed at any time. Meanwhile, European governments are working on new gas infrastructure. Poland and Lithuania are building their own LNG terminals to reduce dependence on Russian pipelines.[27] More important, European governments for years have been mulling over pipelines to circumvent Russia. Last year, the European Union aborted the ambitious Nabucco pipeline project, which would have run from Azerbaijan across Georgia and Turkey to the Bulgarian border. Still, the smaller Trans-Anatolian Pipeline (TANAP) and Trans-Adriatic Pipeline (TAP) are due to be completed by 2020, and the Nabucco failure served as a wakeup call to policymakers in the region.[28]

Table 3: Gazprom Net Sales by Geographic Segment, Gas and Other, 2013

	Gas	Other	Total
Russia	27%	68%	45%
Europe and other	58%	26%	44%
Former Soviet Union	15%	6%	11%
Total (roubles bn)	2,884.8	2,362.8	5,247.6
Total (US$ bn)	83.4	68.3	151.7

Source: Gazprom 2013 financial report. *http://www.gazprom.com/f/posts/07/271326/gazprom-financial-report-2013-en.pdf.*

Russia's "Asia pivot", once an option, is increasingly a necessity. Moscow is exploring other countermeasures to improve its economy and its status in the gas market, including breaking up Gazprom's monopoly over Russia's gas exports; forcing Gazprom to seek more alliances with foreign companies; coordinating with other natural gas exporting countries through the Gas Exporting Countries Forum (GECF); and actively courting investors for new gas pipelines.[29] But without new clients in Asia, these measures are unlikely to be effective.

Key Points of Contention

Although the preconditions for a natural gas supply deal have been n place for some time, it took China and Russia until 2014 to reach a deal. Dating back to 1997, Russia agreed to sell 30 bcm to China and South Korea. In 2006, Presidents Putin and Hu signed an agreement to build two pipelines to allow the annual sale of 80 bcm from Russia to China, followed by a financial cooperation agreement between Gazprom and CNPC. None of these agreements were implemented. The two sides met again in 2009 to explore the possibility of a new supply agreement to ensure delivery of 70 bcm in 2015.[30] In June 2011, five-year negotiations over a 30 bcm supply deal faltered once again.[31]

The causes for the deadlock were complex. Key points of contention included:

- *The price.* Initially, China and Russia tabled prices that were too far apart (as high as $100 per 1,000 cubic meters) for compromise. China demanded prices similar to those it paid to its primary pipeline gas supplier, Turkmenistan. Factoring in longer transport routes, Russia demanded prices equal or above those it charged Europe. An additional question was how to structure the pricing formula to accommodate changing prices in the oil or gas market. Russia favored tying the price to oil, as it has done in its European contracts. Oil is witnessing a more robust price trend than gas. While other negotiators might have made the case for a price based on the gas spot market, China reportedly went a step further, insisting that the price be linked to coal, a formula widely used within China.[32]

- *The shipping route.* Russia wanted to service China from the same gas fields in Western Siberia that it uses for the European market, in order to act as a "swing producer" between the two continents. It would do so by extending existing pipeline infrastructure to meet with China's West-East Pipeline in Xinjiang Autonomous Region, a stretch known as the "Altai route." In October 2009, Gazprom and CNPC in fact inked a framework agreement for the Altai project.[33] However, China appears to have backpedaled, arguing that, since it was already sourcing gas for the West-East Pipeline from Central Asia, it was no longer interested in Russia's proposal. It now wanted Russia to open new gas fields in East Siberia and to ship this gas to northeast China via the "Power of Siberia" route. Northeast China is an area of strategic importance to China's economy that has almost no gas in its energy mix. Although Russia was actually keen to extract gas in East Siberia, it planned to use it for the larger Japanese and Korean gas markets – in conjunction with a Russo-Japanese investment in an LNG port at Vladivostock, and via a pipeline to be built from Russia through North Korea to South Korea.[34]

- *Payment and investment conditions.* A final key area of contention was how China would pay for the gas. Gas is a much riskier asset than oil: producers must contend with high capital costs for extraction, storage, and shipping; consumers face the risk of supply shortages if producers fail to deliver, since gas is less fungible than oil on the world market. In the Sino-Russian deal, payment disputes revolved around three issues: (1) how much China would agree to prepay to support Gazprom's initial investments; (2) whether and what type of "take-or-pay" provision China would accept; and (3) perhaps most important, whether China would be given an equity stake in Gazprom's project to mitigate supply risk and share in the profits.

2. Executing the Deal: Benefits and Risks for China

A simplistic view of the May 2014 deal is that Russia, under political and economic duress, finally acquiesced to Chinese demands. In reality, the talks made progress beginning in 2012 and exacted compromises from both sides. Several important commitments were made in a March 2013 MOU. Judging by the prolonged negotiations at the May summit (which lasted until half past three in the morning, according to President Putin),[35] some contentious issues – particularly price and payment – were only resolved at the last minute.

Key Outcomes and Compromises

(1) Route

For China, the biggest coup was doubtless Russia's willingness to ship the gas via the Power of Siberia route to northeast China. The consultancy Wood MacKenzie predicts that, by 2025, Power of Siberia gas could supply over a quarter of gas demand in northeast China.[36] The outlines of this clause were already agreed to in the March 2013 MOU. A ready explanation for this compromise is that it was a make-or-break provision; unlike pricing, for example, China left Russia no room for negotiation on this point.

A more technical explanation is that Russia came to view a Power of Siberia route co-financed by China as in its own best interest. Like China, Russia envisions a future in which national and transnational pipelines are interconnected into a vast grid, which would improve market efficiencies. Originally, Russia may have relied on Japan and other foreign investors to contribute capital for new pipelines in East Siberia, yet this expectation has not materialized. Japan and Korea lack domestic pipeline infrastructure and so will continue to focus future consumption on LNG.[37] The regime transition in North Korea arguably killed plans to build a gas pipeline from Russia through North Korea to the South.[38]

Gazprom may yet use some of its Power of Siberia shipments to service Japan and Korea. Many energy analysts see the project as a boon to the Vladivostock LNG port, which could receive significant volumes from the Kovyktinskoye fields.[39] Russia may also look to China to liquefy Russian natural gas for export to third markets.[40]

(2) Price

The official price and pricing formula behind the May 2014 contract have not been disclosed (see Appendix Table A-5 for various estimates). Gazprom CEO Alexey Miller earlier called the price a "commercial secret."[41] At face value, though, China seems to have gotten a better deal. With a nominal price of around $350 per 1,000 cubic meters, China is effectively paying less, not more, than Europe for Russian gas. Asian spot market prices hit an all-time high in February 2014 – relative to those prices, China struck an even better bargain (see Table 4).[x]

Table 4: Gas Prices in the World Market and the China-Russia Gas Contract, May 2014

	Sources	$/mmBtu	$/1,000 m3
Asia spot LNG	Spot market index (Reuters, May 21)	$ 14.00	$ 501.20
Gazprom to Europe	2013 average sales price (Reuters, May 21)	$ 10.60	$ 380.00
China-Russia deal	**Consensus estimate**	**$ 9.78**	**$ 350.00**
China from Turkmenistan	Off-take agreement, current price	$ 9.00	$ 322.20
UK spot	Spot market index (Reuters, May 21)	$ 7.70	$ 275.66
U.S. spot	Spot market index (Reuters, May 21)	$ 4.50	$ 161.10

It would be rash to declare China the outright victor in the price talks. President Putin has intimated that the price is partially indexed to oil markets, which would count in Russia's favor; indeed, China has already agreed to such indexing in its smaller Yamal LNG project with Russia (see section below on corollary energy deals).[42] Gazprom has also indicated that it is not going to bend on a principle that it applies to all its sales contracts in Europe.[43]

China may also have agreed to a price that in retrospect will appear too high. Experts predict that, as of next year, vast new supplies of natural gas will hit the world market. U.S. shale producer Cheniere Energy will export gas via the Sabine Pass Terminal in Louisiana, a portion of which will be sold on the open market via British Gas and other companies. More U.S. companies could obtain export licenses in the near future. In East Africa, the world's second-largest gas liquefaction site is being built in Mozambique. In the end, China's NOCs could face a tradeoff: softer prices will lower the cost of spot market imports, at the cost of paying too much for the Russian gas.[44]

---

[x] According to Gordon Kwan, head of oil and gas research at Nomura International Hong Kong Ltd: "The deal is an economic game changer as PetroChina lands an attractive gas deal at a price that carries a 10 percent discount to what EU countries are currently paying, and a 40 percent discount to current LNG prices." Quoted in Aibing Guo, "PetroChina, Utilities Stand to Gain from Russia Gas Deal," Bloomberg, May 22, 2014, via Factiva.

(3) Investment and Payment

Also problematic for China are the payment and investment conditions it has agreed to. At first blush, the Russians appear to have accepted most of the investment risk regarding exploration and transport infrastructure. Gazprom has said it will invest $55 billion, while CNPC will only pre-pay $25 billion. During earlier talks with the Russians, CNPC reportedly tabled a pre-payment offer of $50 billion.[45] China's benefit on the pre-payment side, however, may be offset by its failure to secure an equity stake in the gas fields. At present, there is no indication that it has secured such a stake.[46]

If China did not secure any equity, then this was a significant concession. In Kazakhstan and Turkmenistan, CNPC is a co-investor in much of the oil and gas shipped to China. Some experts in the past have argued that China would not agree to a deal without getting an equity stake, since this would deprive CNPC of lucrative profits, and worse still, expose China to potential supply suspensions. Russia's official projections for future gas production (see Table 5) may be unrealistic, given the scarcity of long-term supply agreements, the potential for delays caused due to economic and political crises, and the technical difficulties of putting into operation huge fields across Russia's far-flung territory.[47]

Table 5: Russian Government Forecast of Future Gas Production by Gas Field
(billions cubic meters)

	2008	2013-2015	2020-2022	2030
Western Siberia	604	586-599	589-592	612-642
Europe	46	54-91	116-119	131-137
Caspian Sea	*0*	*8-20*	*20-22*	*21-22*
Shtokman (Arctic)	*0*	*0-23*	*50-51*	*69-71*
Eastern Siberia	*4*	*9-13*	*9-13*	*26-55*
Far East	9	34-40	65-67	85-87
Sakhalin	*7*	*31-36*	*36-37*	*50-51*
Total gas output	664	685-745	803-837	885-940

Source: Adapted from Rafael Fernández and Enrique Palazuelos, "The Future of Russian Gas Exports to East Asia: Feasibility and Market Implications," *Futures* 43, no. 10 (2011): 1073.

Adding to uncertainty of future deliveries is Russia's domestic gas consumption. Russians consume 70 percent of domestic production, and gas accounts for over half of Russia's primary energy structure. Gazprom has greatly increased the degree of gasification in Russia from 53 percent in 2005 to 64 percent in 2012. If domestic economic growth revives and/or Russia fails to improve its energy efficiencies, domestic needs could divert gas away from export markets.[48] Since gas is heavily subsidized in Russia, Gazprom will prefer to sell abroad, but the Kremlin will be wary of the consequences for domestic stability.

A final compromise worth highlighting is the take-or-pay provision.[49] Although details about the precise level are unknown, this concession may give China little flexibility should gas market conditions change between 2020 and 2050. For example, if China's domestic gas production performs better than expected, China will still have to pay the Russians for gas it may not need. Some energy experts project that a shale revolution in China could dampen Russian exports over the coming decades (see Appendix Table A-6).

Interest Group Politics

Neither China nor Russia is a unitary actor. Different interest groups in each country will greet this deal with different levels of enthusiasm. In China, CNPC's subsidiary Petrochina has recently been the target of far-reaching corruption probes.[xi] The deal may extend an olive branch to the embattled company. The deal will also add to CNPC's substantial portfolio in Eurasia, where it has been much more active than

---

[xi] For more information, see the *USCC 2013 Annual Report*, p.42.

China National Offshore Oil Corporation (CNOOC) and China Petroleum & Chemical Corporation (Sinopec), the country's other NOCs. Although CNPC is likely to benefit from the deal, it may also find it difficult to reconcile future payments to Russia with its ongoing operations in domestic shale production and new LNG facilities. Loans from China's state-owned banks may be necessary to honor future contracts. CNPC may also be upset at its failure to acquire an equity stake in the new Siberian fields: Erica Downs, a leading energy expert at Brookings, argues that Chinese oil companies prefer to have direct access to upstream production overseas, because these are the most profitable part of their business.[50]

CNOOC, the smaller and arguably most efficient of China's NOCs, is the leader in China's LNG segment. It is aggressively building LNG infrastructure. Unlike CNPC, it plays a marginal role in pipeline gas imports, and so cannot hedge between the pipeline and LNG markets.[xii] Producers of other energy sources, such as coal, hydropower, wind, and nuclear, may also oppose the deal. The biggest winners may end up being downstream gas distributors at the municipal level, as well as equipment suppliers who will build out the gas pipelines in China's northeast.[51]

In the case of Russia, the appearance of close coordination among the country's political and economic elites may be deceiving. Some analysts have argued that the Kremlin took the lead in negotiating this deal, without fully considering the impact on the financial health of Gazprom, which now has to figure out how to finance the project.[52] Further, the future price competitiveness of Russia's gas exports to East Asia may hinge on tax breaks and exemptions granted by the Russian government to gas exporters.[xiii] Putin has backed such policies, but other Russian officials have voiced concern about the impact this could have on Russia's fiscal revenue.[53] (Given that natural gas exports only bring in 30 percent of overall oil and gas revenues, there may be more leeway to institute tax breaks than in the oil sector.[54])

3. Broader Motives behind the Agreement

Geopolitical Interests

A lingering question about this deal is whether China could have pushed Russia harder at the bargaining table. China enjoys some advantages: it has many other gas suppliers, is fairly self-reliant, and depends far less on gas for consumption than Russia does for export. At the same time, Russia's relations with Europe are frayed. As described in the previous section, Russia has already been forced to renegotiate contracts with European customers. These tensions have been intensified by the Ukraine crisis. In March, Gazprom decided to no longer subsidize gas exports to Ukraine, and proceeded to charge Ukraine the highest gas prices in Europe. The European Commission interpreted this as a political move to isolate Kiev. Ukraine's disputed gas debt could be as much as $5.2 billion through the end of May, and Gazprom has demanded at least a partial payment.[55] European leaders will also convene in June to discuss diversifying gas imports away from Russia. These actions are particularly controversial, given that the preponderance of Russian gas to Europe flows through Ukraine (see Appendix Table A-7).

Geopolitics may be one factor that explains why China softened its bargaining position. China's former Premier Wen Jiabao stated in 2006 that "energy issues should not be politicized." Notwithstanding this public rhetoric, energy deals today are integral to China's foreign policy. Beijing likely views this gas deal

---

[xii] According to data from 2013, CNOOC accounted for over half of the 34.8 million tons per annum of LNG import capacity in China (operating, under construction, or proposed). Keun-Wook Paik, "The Role of Russian Gas in China's Energy Supply Strategy," *Asia Europe Journal* 11:3 (2013): 328.

[xiii] Russia's tax system has three tiers: a mineral extraction tax, a corporate tax, and export duties on crude oil and products. There has been spirited debate among three government entities – the Ministry of Economic Development, Ministry of Finance, and Ministry of Energy – around tax reform. The Ministry of Energy wants to incentivize production via tax cuts but that would be painful for an economy that relies on oil and gas for more than half of federal budget revenue. Some leeway was granted with a slight reduction of export duties on oil in October 2011, set to extend through 2014, but the Ministry of Energy wants a reduction in the mineral extraction tax. Elena Shadrina and Michael Bradshaw, "Russia's Energy Governance Transitions and Implications for Enhanced Cooperation with China, Japan, and South Korea," *Post-Soviet Affairs* 29:6 (2013): 474-475.

as part of its broader effort to advance security cooperation with Moscow, while countering U.S. power and influence in Central and East Asia.[xiv]

Since President Xi came to power, China and Russia have taken concrete steps to improve security ties along several dimensions. Perhaps the most visible dimension has been military:

- *Joint training exercises.* In May 2014, the PLA Navy and the Russian Federation Navy held "Joint Sea-2014" in the East China Sea, off the coast of Shanghai. Fourteen surface combatants, two submarines, and nine aircraft reportedly participated in the exercise, which included training for joint antisubmarine warfare, joint antisurface warfare, and joint antiair warfare. According to official Chinese media, Chinese and Russian ships during the exercise were mixed together to form "composite formations" for the first time.[56] China and Russia have conducted military drills bilaterally or under the auspices of the Shanghai Cooperation Organization since 2005, but this was only the third naval exercise between the two countries.

- *Russian military exports to China.* Since the 1990s, Russian military exports to China have represented the most important aspect of the two countries' security relationship. Russian firms have reaped significant revenue from the sales, which also helped sustain Russia's struggling defense industries during the 1990s. China's military has been able to acquire advanced weapon systems and technologies that it has been unable to produce at home. Although Moscow's concern over China's record of disregarding intellectual property rights by copying Russian weapon designs has contributed to a decline in Russian arms sales to China since the mid-2000s, the two sides reportedly are close to finalizing their largest-ever weapon sale, which will likely include advanced Russian fighter aircraft, attack submarines, and air defense systems.[57]

Alongside these military activities, China and Russia have intensified bilateral diplomacy:

- *More high-level meetings and interest in a strategic partnership.* The May summit was the seventh meeting between President Xi and President Putin since March 2013.[58] President Xi chose Russia as the destination for his first official foreign trip as China's president in March 2013. During the visit, China and Russia agreed to "resolutely support each other in efforts to protect national sovereignty, security, and development interests." President Xi called for the two sides to "closely coordinate in international regional affairs," and President Putin said "the strategic partnership between us is of great importance on both a bilateral and global scale."[59] President Xi returned to Russia later in 2013 for the G-20 summit and again in 2014 to attend the opening ceremony of the Sochi Olympics. President Xi's decision to attend the ceremony, despite mounting security concerns and the decision by leaders from most major Western countries to skip the event, was hailed by both Chinese and Russian official media as a major event in China-Russia relations.[60]

- *Coordinated diplomacy on select issues.* Russia and China have gone to great lengths not to contradict one another on their respective interpretations of national sovereignty. The two countries have vetoed several UNSC resolutions on Syria, doing so for the fourth time on May 23, following the bilateral summit in Beijing.[61][xv] On May 14, a week ahead of President Putin's trip to China, the Russian Foreign Ministry reiterated the importance of close UNSC cooperation in the bilateral relationship, referring expressly to Syria.[62] China also has moderated its typical "non-interference policy" talking points to accommodate Russia. Despite China's claims to respect other countries' sovereignty and stated opposition to interference in the internal affairs of other

---

[xiv] Wang Jisi, a professor at Peking University and an influential policy thinker, has advocated China's "March Westward" to source energy, develop the poor western regions of China, promote domestic stability, and spread geopolitical influence in a strategic region at a time when the United States is pivoting to Asia. Wang Jisi, "'Marching Westwards': The Rebalancing of China's Geostrategy," *Center for International and Strategic Studies Report* 73 (October 2012), p.1.
[xv] China has never used its UNSC veto this many times on one issue. See United Nations database. *http://www.un.org/depts/dhl/resguide/scact_veto_en.shtml.*

countries, China has not opposed Russia's decision to send troops to Crimea. A commentary in official Chinese media explained, "It is quite understandable when Putin said his country retained the right to protect its interests and Russian-speakers living in Ukraine." Instead of opposing Russia's move, the article argues the West should "respect Russia's unique role in mapping out the future of Ukraine." [63] Moreover, in March China abstained from voting on a resolution condemning the contentious referendum in Crimea, which many argue was rigged by Russia. President Putin thanked China for its abstention, saying Beijing's leadership took "the entire historical dimension" into account when looking at the situation in Ukraine. Beijing has also spoken out against placing Western sanctions on Russia. [64]

The recent improvement in security ties was reinforced at the May summit in Beijing, which formed part of the Conference on Interaction and Confidence Building Measures in Asia (CICA). In his opening remarks at the conference on May 21, President Xi said "the issues of Asia can only be solved by Asians and the security of Asia can only be maintained by Asians....[Asia] need[s] to adopt an innovative security concept, establish a new regional security cooperation architecture, and jointly build a road for security in Asia that is shared by all and is a win-win for all." [65][xv] Although the CICA has 24 member nations – including South Korea, Thailand, Turkey, and Iran – China and Russia dominate the agenda. (The United States is not a member of the CICA.) The two sides also signed a joint statement stating that the "international community should collaborate on the basis of mutual respect and benefit," a point reiterated by President Putin in a telegram addressed to SPIEF. [66]

Nevertheless, it is unlikely that these moves will eliminate longstanding bilateral tensions driven by historical animosity, mutual suspicion, and the potential for conflict over territory and resources. China almost certainly will not attempt to establish a formal military alliance with Russia and probably will continue to prioritize its security relations with Washington over those it has with Moscow. China's actions on Crimea and Syria may have more to do with China's broader security and foreign policy objectives than its efforts to bolster relations with Russia. Russia, for its part, is concerned about aiding the build-up of China's military-industrial complex, as well as China's rising influence over Russia's vast far eastern territories, which are rich in resources but increasingly devoid of people. [67] Russia is concerned by China's increasing naval activity in the Sea of Okhotsk, an important military and economic maritime area for Moscow. Russia has also supported Vietnam through arms sales, joint construction of nuclear reactors, and increased energy cooperation in the South China Sea, large parts of which are claimed by China." [68]

Cooperation in the context of the Shanghai Cooperation Organization has been limited as well, in part because Russia views the organization as a forum for China to facilitate energy deals with Central Asian countries. The inauguration of the Central Asia-China pipeline marked the first major diversion of former Soviet Republic gas resources outside the Soviet legacy Gazprom pipeline network, and greatly enhanced Turkmenistan's bargaining leverage vis-à-vis Gazprom. [69] It appears that Russia has since opted for Plan B, preferring that gas from Central Asia flow east to China rather than west to Europe, as this will have a lesser impact on its overall bargaining leverage. [70]

A Maturing Energy Partnership

The gas supply deal also builds on maturing energy ties between China and Russia, starting with oil. In July of last year, Russia's Rosneft agreed to more than double its oil shipments to China in a long-term supply agreement. In many ways, the May 2014 gas deal mirrors the 2009 Rosneft-CNPC oil off-take agreement: (1) Russia at the time was under economic duress due to the global financial crisis, with Rosneft finding it difficult to meet its payment obligations; (2) Moscow's strategy of hedging Japan against China as an alternative client fell through due to Japanese reluctance; (3) Russia agreed to ship the oil to China via an eastern instead of a western route; and (4) China agreed to an off-take agreement at a low

---

[xvi] For the full text of this speech, see Xi Jinping, "Full Text of PRC President Xi Jinping's Speech at Fourth Summit of Conference on Interaction and Confidence-Building Measures in Asia in Shanghai on 21 May" Xinhua (Chinese edition), May 21, 2014. Open Source Center translation. ID: CHR2014052139501046.

price, in return for not requiring an equity stake in the oilfields, thereby acquiescing to Russian sensitivities about foreign ownership in the energy sector.[71]

Another important corollary to the gas deal is China's partnership with other Russian gas producers. When President Putin decided last year to break Gazprom's gas export monopoly, two new agreements with China quickly resulted:

- *Yamal LNG project (June 2013; May 2014).* In June 2013, Novatek, Russia's second-largest gas producer, signed a deal to supply 3 million tons of LNG per year to China over a 20-year period. The gas will be sourced from the $27 billion Yamal LNG project, due to be launched in 2017 with 5.5 million tons of annual capacity. CNPC, alongside French energy company Total, was permitted to acquire 20 percent in Yamal.[72] The deal was formalized on May 20 of this year, during the Russia-China summit, where it was revealed that the price would be determined by a formula linked to the Japan Customs-cleared Crude (JCC) oil index. The Yamal LNG consortium also signed a deal with China Development Bank, China's state-owned policy bank, to provide policy financing to the project.[73] Intriguingly, three days later, when the $400 billion gas supply deal had been completed, Gazprom's trading unit Gazprom Marketing and Trading signed a deal to source 3 million tons of LNG from the Yamal project.[74] In other words, while Gazprom has been reluctant to let China invest in its own project, it is lending support to a smaller Russian gas project in which CNPC has a stake.

- *Rosneft-CNPC deal (October 2013).* Russia's energy giant Rosneft, which produces both oil and gas, has been keen to enter the gas market alongside Gazprom, particularly in the LNG segment, which Gazprom has been slow to enter. Rosneft has some 7 trillion cubic meters in gas reserves in eastern Siberia and predicts long-term production potential at 200 bcm per annum (more than the total 160 bcm that Gazprom exported to Europe last year). In October of last year, Rosneft managed to secure rights to ship seaborne LNG abroad for the first time. Right after this permission was granted, Rosneft Chairman Igor Sechin signed a strategic MOU with CNPC to jointly develop Rosneft's East Siberian hydrocarbon fields. Sechin has said Rosneft could tap into Gazprom's Power of Siberia gas pipeline to China if allowed access, but that many other options are available, such as building separate pipelines to China. [75]

In addition to these joint gas projects, Russia and China also signed commercial deals at the May summit to co-invest in downstream oil and gas projects:

- *Shanghai Chemical Industry Park.* Sinopec and Russia's SIBUR signed a joint venture agreement to produce nitrile rubber at the Shanghai Chemical Industry Park. Sinopec will own 74.9 percent of the shares in the joint venture, and SIBUR 25.1 percent. The two sides agreed to pursue opportunities in natural gas processing.[76]

- *Tianjin oil refinery.* Rosneft and CNPC agreed to launch a joint venture oil refinery in Tianjin municipality, a fast-growing center of China's petrochemical industry. The project will be located in the Binhai New Area, one of China's strategic development zones. Rosneft will be the sole oil supplier for this refinery, which will have a capacity of 16 million tons when it launches in 2019. The second stage involves the creation of a network of petrol stations in China, which will operate under the name Rosneft and CNPC.[77] In line with China's law on joint ventures, Rosneft will be limited to a 49 percent minority stake. Most of the production capacity will be used to produce light petroleum products; in addition to LNG and fuel gas, it will produce aromatic hydrocarbons and petrochemicals such as polypropylene, which are in high demand in China's chemical industry.[78]

- *Potential for Russia to acquire Chinese technology for shale oil extraction.* Although Russia holds large shale oil resources, it relies heavily on foreign technology. [79] According to Genady Timchenko, Russia's lead negotiator on the China trip (and co-owner of the gas producer Novatek), Russia will increase purchases of shale oil extraction equipment from China if U.S. and European firms continue to scale back technology transfers as part of ongoing sanctions against

Russia.[80] Xia Yishan, Chairman of the China Center for Energy Strategy Studies, stated that China can "manufacture all kinds of exploration facilities and drilling platforms—and our prices are 50 to 60 percent lower than European and U.S. products of equal quality."[81]

Non-Energy Economic Interests

The gas deal can also be viewed as one facet of maturing economic ties between China and Russia. Over 30 commercial deals were signed at the May summit, not only in energy, but also infrastructure logistics, manufacturing, and finance. Most of these signings occurred on May 20, a day before the $400 billion gas contract was concluded. Several have long-term, strategic implications:

- *Currency swaps.* Russia's second largest lender Vneshtcrgbank (VTB) signed a cooperation agreement with Bank of China to use Russian and Chinese currency in bilateral transactions, and thus avoid using U.S. dollars for investment banking, inter-bank loans, trade finance, and capital markets transactions.[82] The deal follows preparatory talks held between Chinese Vice-Premier Zhang Gaoli and his Russian counterpart in early May. Vice-Premier Zhang stated at that meeting that "financial cooperation between China and Russia is growing as local currency settlement in two-way trade increases. Consultations on a package of currency swaps are ongoing."[83]

- *Partnering on rail, power distribution, and port projects.* Three deals were signed that in the future could better connect the two countries' infrastructure networks, and potentially complement the gas pipeline construction in East Siberia. Russian Railways and China Railway Corporation agreed to develop rail infrastructure at border crossings and the routes leading up to them to increase the capacity of railways, the volume of international traffic in the region, and the size of terminal and storage facilities along the main routes. If realized, the deal could spur more container traffic from China to Europe.[84] China's railway companies are already helping to construct rail systems through Kyrgyzstan to Uzbekistan, and a high-speed train between China and Kazakhstan.[85] In the power sector, Russian Grids and the State Grid Corporation of China will consider building ultra-high voltage power transmission lines from Russia to China, accompanied by an underground substation in Russia.[86] Not least, the provincial government of Jilin Province, in northeast China, and Summa Group, Russia's largest port operator, signed a cooperation framework agreement to build a multipurpose shipping port at Zarubino, a port on the Pacific coast in Russian territory, just east of Jilin. This will ease the shipping of goods from landlocked Jilin to neighboring Japan and Korea; currently most goods from the northeast are exported further south via Dalian.[87]

- *Joint development of a wide-body long-haul passenger aircraft.* China and Russia are both keen to compete in the passenger aircraft market, which is currently dominated by Airbus and Boeing. In 2012, Russia's United Aircraft Corporation (UAC) and Commercial Aircraft Corporation of China (COMAC) signed an MOU to jointly develop and manufacture a wide-body, long-haul aircraft that could eventually become one of the most large-scale projects of international cooperation in the aviation sector. At the May summit, UAC confirmed that it had already completed its conceptual design and corresponding economic and technical feasibility studies, ahead of this summer's deadline. A second cooperation project involves joint development of new helicopters for Chinese military and civilian needs, which are to have twice the deadweight lift capacity of the MI-26 that the People's Liberation Army (PLA) currently uses.[88]

- *Chinese automotive assembly in Russia.* Great Wall Motor, China's largest sport utility vehicle producer, signed an agreement to invest over $500 million to build a vehicle production plant south of Moscow, the company's first full-vehicle assembly plant overseas.[89] The plant is set to launch in 2017, with production capacity of 150,000 units.[90] China's indigenous automakers have struggled of late: domestically, they are being outcompeted by foreign brands; overseas, demand for Chinese cars in emerging markets like Russia and Iran is slowing. Viewed in this context, the deal indicates Beijing's vote of confidence in its auto sector and the health of Russia's consumer economy.

Besides these sector-level interests, both countries have identified development of the east – meaning East Siberia and northeast China – as a strategic priority. China's northeastern rustbelt bore the brunt of government-enforced reductions in manufacturing capacity in the late 1990s and early 2000s. The Power of Siberia pipeline could spur local development through large infrastructure projects and a diversification of the region's energy mix. The CNPC-Rosneft refinery in Tianjin and the planned port at Zarubino will also help China's northeast. Across the border, the gas deal will spur development in Russia's Far East, according to Russian Deputy Energy Minister Kirill Molodtsov.[91] China's Vice-Premier Zhang Gaoli has asked the Russian government to aid Chinese enterprises in investing in special economic zones in that part of Russia. Several Chinese firms are already investing there.[92]

Although broad-based economic interests likely helped facilitate the gas deal, the Sino-Russian economic partnership is built on shaky ground. Both countries are currently experiencing an economic downturn, but recessionary pressures are much greater in Russia, and are compounded by the threat of more sanctions. At the eighteenth annual St. Petersburg International Economic Forum (SPIEF), held on May 22-24, Russia's political and business elite trumpeted the country's new deals with China to boost confidence among the foreign investors in attendance.[93] But it is far from certain whether the litany of "strategic cooperation agreements" will bear fruit. In the aviation sector, for instance, Russia has lost its competitive edge and will find it hard to co-develop a plane with China that is capable of competing with Airbus and Boeing.

As in the gas sector, there is an inherent asymmetry between the two countries' economic clout. The *Economist* predicts China's GDP to grow by 7.3 percent this year, Russia's only by 1.2 percent.[94] China is Russia's largest trade partner, but Russia is only China's ninth-largest. Bilateral trade is premised on a commodities-for-manufactures pattern, akin to China's trade with commodity exporters in Latin America. According to China's customs data, Russian exports to China declined by 10 percent last year, and Russia ran a trade deficit equivalent to 11 percent of bilateral trade.[xvii]

Russia is also desperate to attract more Chinese foreign investments. Economic Development Minister Alexey Ulyukaev expects China's investments in Russia to rise by 700 percent between now and 2020.[95] China's Vice-Premier Zhang stated on May 9 that China will aim to boost Greenfield, M&A, and equity investment in Russia via the bilateral Russia-China Investment Fund launched in 2012, with an eye toward Russia's Far East.[xviii][96] However, Chinese companies have been reluctant to enter Russia other than through state-directed projects. And while Russian public opinion about China has greatly improved,[xix] many Russian companies are still wary of Chinese takeovers.

[xvii] Data from China's General Administration of Customs, via CEIC data.

[xviii] In September 2010, Russian Finance Minister Alexei Kudrin announced that the government was preparing to sell $10 billion worth of state-owned assets per year for approximately five years. Nine months later, Moscow founded the Russian Direct Investment Fund (RDIF), a private equity vehicle under Russia's state-owned bank Vnesheconombank (VEB). RDIF's principal aim is to counteract the sharp drop in Russia's FDI inflows by courting foreign investors, both sovereign and private. RDIF is mandated to secure co-investment that as a minimum matches Russia's own commitment. China Investment Corp. (CIC), China's official sovereign wealth fund, became the first foreign investor to commit to RDIF, doing so through the creation of a Russia-China Investment Fund (RCIF). Earlier, in September 2009, CIC took a 45 percent interest in Russia's state-owned Nobel Oil Group. For more information, see Iacob Koch-Weser and Owen Haake, "China Investment Corporation: Recent Developments in Performance, Strategy, and Governance" (Washington, DC: U.S.-China Economic and Security Review Commission, June 2013), pp.26, 30-31.

[xix] Public opinion about China appears to have improved in Russia. A poll published in April by polling institute FOM found that about three-quarters of Russians believe that a relationship between the two countries is beneficial. About 57 percent of those polled believe that a strong China does not pose a threat to Russian interests; in 2009, public sentiment was reversed: 39 percent did not fear China, while 44 percent saw it as a threat. Deutsche Welle, "Moscow Aims to Trade Energy for Chinese Investment in Russia," May 21, 2014 via Factiva.

4. Strategic Implications for the United States, Europe, and Japan

The Impact on Global Gas Markets and U.S. Production

Research on China's global resource acquisitions often asks whether China is "locking up" supply by taking direct ownership of overseas assets or securing long-term off-take agreements with key producers. In the worst-case scenario, this could give rise to a zero-sum pursuit of finite resources. A related concern is that the Chinese government might one day create an "oligopsony": China could use its preeminent role in resource markets, combined with government control over energy companies, to manipulate resource supplies and prices for economic or security purposes.[xx] Examples of "locking up" supply might be Turkmenistan and Kazakhstan, where China now owns substantial equity in oil and gas fields.

Critics counter that this dark view of China's behavior misrepresents the facts. China usually diversifies supply by investing in new production in peripheral regions. In most cases, global markets have become too liquid and sophisticated to be manipulated by a single country. Driven increasingly by profit incentives, Chinese state-owned enterprises are more likely to pursue their own interests. If anything, the argument goes, China may exercise monopoly power over its domestic resources, as it has done by placing export restrictions on rare earths.[xxi]

How does the Sino-Russian gas supply deal figure in this debate? While the deal is not cause for alarm, it is important to tease out its varying impacts on different gas suppliers and consumers. For U.S. gas producers, the deal is primarily a long-term concern. In the short run, U.S. gas exports to China are likely to continue growing from a low base. Cheniere Energy, which has received an export license from the U.S. government, will begin exporting LNG from Louisiana next year, much of which will go to Asia. Although the China-Russia pipeline deal could contribute to softening LNG prices worldwide, Cheniere and its downstream distributors will still make a sizable profit from the gap between U.S. and Asian gas prices. Analysts at Societe Generale SA and Sanford C. Bernstein & Co. warn, however, that the Sino-Russian deal could make long-term investors warier of taking on high-cost LNG projects in the United States and elsewhere. If these new LNG projects come online in the next five to ten years, concurrent with the Power of Siberia pipeline, low gas prices at that point could reduce the return on investment.[97]

The immediate impact on Europe will likely be limited. Gazprom will ship to China from fields in eastern Siberia, while Europe is mainly fed by projects in western Siberia, a point substantiated by energy analysts from the Oxford Institute for Energy Studies.[98] According to Laszlo Varro, head of the International Energy Agency's Gas, Coal and Power Market Division, the deal could even benefit Europe competitively as it means China will purchase less gas on the LNG spot market, leaving more available for Europe.[99]

In the long run, however, European gas consumers could be affected by Russia's "Asia pivot." One projection for the year 2030 suggests that if Russian gas exports to Asia reach 70 bcm, and Russia's domestic consumption continues to grow at its current pace, then Russian sales to Europe would decrease from their current level of 180 bcm to about 149 bcm. Even if Russia's domestic consumption slows, sales to Asia could still keep Russian sales to Europe at current levels by 2030.[100]

For Japan, the deal likewise presents opportunities and risks. Japan imported three times as much gas as China in 2012, and has a much higher rate of import reliance. Following the Fukushima incident in 2011, the government has been eager to substitute more gas-fired power for nuclear energy. In a bid to secure long-term supplies, Japanese companies have already co-invested in Russian oil and gas projects on Sakhalin Island. Between 2008 and 2013, Japan increased its LNG imports from Russia from zero to 8.6 million metric tons – almost all of that supply came from Sakhalin-2.[101] Japan may benefit from the Sino-

---

[xx] For an elaboration of this theory, see Dambisa F. Moyo, *Winner Take All: China's Race for Resources and What It Means for the World* (New York, NY: Basic Books, 2012), Chapter 6.

[xxi] For an elaboration of this theory, see Theodore H. Moran. *China's Strategy to Secure Natural Resources: Risks, Dangers, and Opportunities*. Vol. 92. Washington, DC: Peterson Institute, 2010.

Russian gas deal if some of the gas from the new East Siberian fields is liquefied and shipped to Japanese ports.

Nonetheless, like Europe, Japan cannot factor out risks. Gazprom has not had a smooth relationship with its Japanese partners. Gazprom attempted to prevent the construction of a pipeline to the island of Hokkaido from Sakhalin-1, and also forced the reduction of shares held by Mitsui and Mitsubishi in Sakhalin-2, to grant Gazprom a majority stake (51 percent) in the consortium.[102] The supply of Sakhalin gas from the Vladivostok project (to be commissioned in 2018) is also uncertain now, as Russia's plans to pipe more gas to China could absorb most of its near-term capital. In future, there could also be a scenario in which Russia must decide between shipping gas to the Vladivostock facility or to Chinese pipelines.[103]

Geopolitical Implications for Dealings with Russia

On May 21, U.S. Secretary of State John Kerry, referring to links between the Sino-Russian gas deal and the Ukraine crisis, stated: "We don't see any relationship whatsoever to an agreement with respect to gas and energy supplies between Russia and China that they've been working on for 10 years…. This isn't a sudden response to what's been going on."[104] Motives aside, Russia cannot in any way use the deal to threaten Europe: initial shipments to China in 2019 will amount to less than a quarter of what Russia sent to Europe last year.

Nonetheless, it is hard to ignore the timing of the deal. It occurred four days prior to the Ukrainian presidential elections, in which evidence of interference at the polls in Eastern Ukraine led some U.S. lawmakers to call for more sanctions against Russia.[105] The deal also came ahead of the G7 Summit and President Barak Obama's trip to Poland.[106] A $400 billion gas deal with China, combined with the other bilateral commercial deals described, may mitigate the impact of Western economic sanctions. The deal has also been symbolically important, by making Russia's elites seem less isolated and giving positive publicity to Gazprom CEO Miller, who has been targeted by sanctions. Deputy Foreign Minister Alexei Meshkov told journalists at SPIEF that "Russia's active cooperation with China will spur Europe's interest in building a mutually beneficial partnership with Moscow."[107] Alexei Pushkov, a Kremlin ally who heads the international affairs committee in the parliament's lower house, argued that the deal is of "strategic significance" because it signals to President Obama that he "should give up the policy of isolating Russia."[108]

Moreover, the agreement with China was sealed just as Gazprom prepared to negotiate future gas shipments to the Ukraine. Ukraine depends heavily on Russia not only for discounted gas, which it uses for its domestic industries, but also as an export market for steel and heavy machinery. If Russia cuts off gas to Ukraine, neither Europe nor the United States can export enough gas to Ukraine to make up for the shortfall.[109] With China now buying Russian gas supplies, Moscow could exert further pressure on Kiev, with less concern about upsetting its European clients.

Appendix Tables and Figures

Table A-1: Composition of China's Energy Production and Consumption, 1995–2011

Production

	Coal	Crude Oil	Natural Gas	Hydro Power, Nuclear Power & Other			
				Total	Hydro	Nuclear	Other
1995	75.3	16.6	1.9	6.2	5.8	0.4	0.0
2000	73.2	17.2	2.7	6.9	6.4	0.5	0.0
2005	77.6	12.0	3.0	7.4	6.5	0.9	0.0
2006	77.8	11.4	3.4	7.5	6.6	0.8	0.1
2007	77.8	10.8	3.7	7.8	6.7	0.9	0.2
2008	76.8	10.5	4.1	8.6	7.5	0.9	0.3
2009	77.3	9.9	4.1	8.7	7.3	0.8	0.6
2010	76.6	9.8	4.2	9.4	7.8	0.8	0.9
2011	77.8	9.1	4.3	8.8	n.a.	n.a.	n.a.

Consumption

	Coal	Crude Oil	Natural Gas	Hydro Power, Nuclear Power & Other			
				Total	Hydro	Nuclear	Other
1995	74.6	17.5	1.8	6.1	5.7	0.4	0.0
2000	69.2	22.2	2.2	6.4	5.9	0.4	0.0
2005	70.8	19.8	2.6	6.8	5.9	0.8	0.1
2006	71.1	19.3	2.9	6.7	5.9	0.7	0.1
2007	71.1	18.8	3.3	6.8	5.9	0.8	0.1
2008	70.3	18.3	3.7	7.7	6.7	0.8	0.2
2009	70.4	17.9	3.9	7.8	6.5	0.8	0.5
2010	68.0	19.0	4.4	8.6	7.1	0.7	0.8
2011	68.4	18.6	5.0	8.0	n.a.	n.a.	n.a.

Source: China National Bureau of Statistics, via CEIC data.

Table A-2.1: Global Gas Exports by Region and Major Exporter, 2008–2012

	2008	2009	2010	2011	2012	Change in share (%) '08-'12	CAGR (%) '08-'12
World (cubic feet billions)	**34,152**	**31,776**	**35,167**	**37,111**	**36,722**		**1.8%**
Eurasia	32.3%	27.6%	26.8%	28.7%	27.2%	-5.0%	-2.4%
Turkmenistan	*5.0%*	*2.0%*	*2.5%*	*4.4%*	*4.4%*	*-0.6%*	*-1.3%*
Russia	*24.2%*	*22.2%*	*21.1%*	*21.6%*	*20.1%*	*-4.1%*	*1.8%*
Europe	20.0%	21.3%	21.0%	19.1%	21.1%	1.1%	3.2%
Norway	*9.9%*	*10.8%*	*10.1%*	*9.2%*	*10.6%*	*0.7%*	*3.7%*
Netherlands	*6.4%*	*6.2%*	*6.0%*	*5.3%*	*5.8%*	*-0.6%*	*-0.5%*
Middle East	8.2%	10.3%	12.9%	14.9%	15.0%	6.7%	18.2%
Qatar	*5.9%*	*7.6%*	*9.6%*	*11.4%*	*11.6%*	*5.7%*	*20.8%*
North America	13.4%	13.7%	12.6%	12.9%	12.9%	-0.5%	0.8%
Canada	*10.5%*	*10.3%*	*9.3%*	*8.8%*	*8.5%*	*-2.0%*	*-3.5%*
United States	*2.8%*	*3.4%*	*3.2%*	*4.1%*	*4.4%*	*1.6%*	*13.9%*
Asia & Oceania	11.0%	11.8%	11.9%	11.4%	11.0%	-0.1%	1.7%
Australia	*1.9%*	*2.3%*	*2.4%*	*2.6%*	*2.5%*	*0.6%*	*8.9%*
Malaysia	*3.2%*	*3.4%*	*3.2%*	*3.1%*	*3.1%*	*0.0%*	*1.4%*
Indonesia	*3.7%*	*3.8%*	*4.1%*	*3.7%*	*3.4%*	*-0.4%*	*-0.9%*
Africa	11.8%	11.6%	11.3%	9.3%	9.4%	-2.4%	-3.7%
Algeria	*6.1%*	*5.9%*	*5.6%*	*4.7%*	*4.7%*	*-1.4%*	*-4.5%*
Central and South America	3.3%	3.6%	3.6%	3.7%	3.4%	0.2%	3.2%

Source: U.S. Energy Information Administration. Staff calculations.

Table A-2.2: Global Gas Imports by Region and Major Importer, 2008–2012

	2008	2009	2010	2011	2012	Change in share (%) '08-'12	CAGR (%) '08-'12
World (cubic feet billions)	**35,403**	**32,581**	**35,766**	**37,430**	**36,967**		**1.1%**
Europe	46.1%	48.7%	46.6%	44.1%	43.3%	-2.8%	-0.5%
Germany	*9.2%*	*10.2%*	*8.8%*	*8.5%*	*8.3%*	*-0.8%*	*-1.3%*
Italy	*7.7%*	*7.5%*	*7.4%*	*6.6%*	*6.5%*	*-1.2%*	*-3.1%*
United Kingdom	*3.6%*	*4.5%*	*5.3%*	*5.0%*	*4.7%*	*1.0%*	*7.7%*
France	*4.9%*	*5.1%*	*4.8%*	*4.5%*	*4.3%*	*-0.6%*	*-2.1%*
Spain	*4.1%*	*4.0%*	*3.6%*	*3.3%*	*3.3%*	*-0.7%*	*-3.7%*
Ukraine	*6.4%*	*2.9%*	*3.6%*	*4.2%*	*3.1%*	*-3.3%*	*-15.4%*
Asia & Oceania	18.7%	20.2%	21.3%	24.2%	26.1%	7.5%	10.0%
Japan	*9.5%*	*10.1%*	*9.8%*	*11.0%*	*11.6%*	*2.1%*	*6.3%*
South Korea	*3.7%*	*3.7%*	*4.3%*	*4.4%*	*4.6%*	*0.9%*	*6.5%*
China	*0.4%*	*0.8%*	*1.6%*	*3.0%*	*4.0%*	*3.5%*	*74.4%*
North America	14.2%	15.1%	14.1%	13.9%	13.6%	-0.6%	-0.1%
Canada	*1.6%*	*2.2%*	*2.2%*	*3.0%*	*3.0%*	*1.4%*	*18.4%*
United States	*11.3%*	*11.5%*	*10.5%*	*9.3%*	*8.5%*	*-2.8%*	*-5.8%*
Eurasia	16.4%	10.5%	11.7%	11.4%	10.5%	-5.8%	-9.5%
Central and South America	1.6%	1.7%	2.3%	2.4%	3.0%	1.4%	18.2%
Middle East	2.6%	3.4%	3.4%	3.4%	2.8%	0.2%	3.2%
Africa	0.5%	0.5%	0.5%	0.6%	0.7%	0.2%	10.3%

Source: U.S. Energy Information Administration. Staff calculations.

Table A-3: Global Gas Reserves by Region
(trillions cubic meters)

	Trillion cubic meters		Share of world (%)	
	Proven reserves	Additional remaining resources	Proven reserves	Additional remaining resources
Middle East	80.5	56.6	43.0%	9.2%
Eurasia	54.7	133.1	29.2%	21.6%
Asia-Pacific	15.5	121.8	8.3%	19.7%
Africa	14.5	85.0	7.7%	13.8%
North America	10.8	99.1	5.8%	16.1%
South America	7.6	79.3	4.1%	12.8%
Europe	3.7	42.5	2.0%	6.9%
TOTAL	187.3	617.3	100.0%	100.0%

Source: Adapted from Sergey Paltsev, "Scenarios for Russia's Natural Gas Exports to 2050," *Energy Economics* 42 (2014): 263.

Table A-4: Russia's Northeast Asia Oriented Gas Projects (as of October 2013)

Project	Companies	Status	Pipeline/LNG
Operational			
Sakhalin-1	Exxon Neftegas Ltd, Rosneft, SMNG, ONGC	Gas exports by pipeline to local market since 2005, by November 2012, 10 bcm delivered	Pipeline
Sakhalin-2	Gazprom, Shell, Mitsui, Mitsubishi	Capacity of 15 bcm since 2009	Pipeline + LNG
Under Development			
Sakhalin-3 (Kirinskiy block)	Gazprom	Production starts in 2013; to connect with Vladivostock	Pipeline
Sakhalin-3 (Veninsky block)	Rosneft and Sinopec	Still in exploration phase	Pipeline
Planned			
Power of Siberia	Gazprom, Irkutsk regional government, and OGK-3	Pipeline linking Kovytka and Chayanda gas fields to SVK pipeline (initial capacity 38 bcm commissioned by 2017 with potential expansion to 61 bcm)	Pipeline
Vladivostock LNG plant	Gazprom	21 bcm capacity, construction scheduled to start in 2013, $7.3 billion investment, commissioning 2018	LNG
Expansion of Sakhalin-2	Gazprom, Shell, Mitsui, Mitsubishi	Construction of a third train with additional 7 bcm, aiming for commissioning in 2018	LNG
Sakhalin-1 LNG plant	Rosneft and ExxonMobil	To be supplied by Sakhalin-1 and Sakhalin-3 (Veninisky), commissioning in 2016	LNG
Yamal LNG	Novatek (80%) and total (20%)	21 bcm capacity based on South Tambeyskoye field, $20 billion investment, commissioning 2016	LNG

Source: Adapted from Elena Shadrina and Michael Bradshaw, "Russia's Energy Governance Transitions and Implications for Enhanced Cooperation with China, Japan, and South Korea," *Post-Soviet Affairs* 29:6 (2013): 487.

Table A-5: Estimates of the Final Price in the May 2014 Gas Deal

Price		Sources
$/mmBtu	$/1,000 m3	
$ 9.67	$ 346.19	Gazprom source (anonymous) (Reuters, May 21)
$ 9.78	$ 350.00	- Arithmetic: $400 bn, 38 bcm, 30 years - Russian Energy Minister Novak: "stated prices are close to the contract" (Interfax, May 23)
>$9.78	>$350.00	"Experts say it could be significantly more than $350" (RIA Novosti, May 21)
$ 10.61	$ 380.00	Arithmetic: With consideration of a five-year period of increasing shipments (Reuters, May 21)

Table A-6: Forecast of Russian Natural Gas Export Scenarios to 2050
(billions cubic meters)

	Volume (bcm)					CAGR (%)	Share	
	2010	2020	2030	2040	2050	'10-'50	2010	2050
Reference Scenario								
Europe	186.9	235.0	246.4	249.2	240.7	0.6%	93.0%	88.3%
Asia	14.2	34.0	65.1	87.8	124.6	5.6%	7.0%	12.8%
Total	201.1	266.2	311.5	337.0	365.3	1.5%		
Asia Gas Policy Scenario								
Europe	186.9	220.9	201.1	206.7	223.7	0.5%	93.0%	84.8%
Asia	14.2	39.6	124.6	158.6	181.2	6.6%	7.0%	15.2%
Total	201.1	260.5	325.6	365.3	404.9	1.8%		
Cheap Shale Gas in China Scenario								
Europe	186.9	235.0	232.2	206.7	181.2	-0.1%	93.0%	87.4%
Asia	14.2	34.0	65.1	42.5	39.6	2.6%	7.0%	12.6%
Total	201.1	269.0	297.3	249.2	220.9	0.2%		

Source: Adapted from Sergey Paltsev, "Scenarios for Russia's Natural Gas Exports to 2050," *Energy Economics* 42 (2014): 268-269.

Table A-7: Russia's European Pipelines
(billions cubic meters)

Pipeline	Capacity (bcm)
Operational	
Ukraine	138.8
Belarus	31.1
NordStream (directly to Germany via Baltic)	53.8
BlueStream (to Turkey)	14.2
Subtotal	237.9
Proposed	
South Stream (Trans-Caspian)	62.3
NordStream II and III (directly to Germany via Baltic)	31.1
Yamal Europe (via Belarus and Poland)	31.1
Subtotal	124.6
TOTAL	362.5

Source: Adapted from Sergey Paltsev, "Scenarios for Russia's Natural Gas Exports to 2050," *Energy Economics* 42 (2014): 264-265.

Endnotes

[1] BBC, "Putin Praises Russia-China Gas Deal as Largest Ever," May 21, 2014, via Factiva.

[2] Paul J. Saunders, "The Not-So-Mighty Russia-China Gas Deal," *The National Interest*, May 23, 2014. *http://nationalinterest.org/feature/the-not-so-mighty-russia-china-gas-deal-10518?page=2*.

[3] Morena Skalamera, "Pipeline Pivot: Why Russia and China Are Poised to Make Energy History" (Cambridge, MA: Harvard Kennedy School, Belfer Center for Science and International Affairs, May 2014).

[4] François Godement and Chi Kong Chyong, "Russia and China's Gas Deal: Ignore the Hype," *European Council on Foreign Relations*, May 23, 2014. *http://ecfr.eu/blog/entry/russia_and_chinas_gas_deal_ignore_the_hype#sthash.FSumkovj.dpuf*.

[5] Morena Skalamera, "Pipeline Pivot: Why Russia and China Are Poised to Make Energy History" (Cambridge, MA: Harvard Kennedy School, Belfer Center for Science and International Affairs, May 2014), p.1.

[6] Morena Skalamera, "Pipeline Pivot: Why Russia and China Are Poised to Make Energy History" (Cambridge, MA: Harvard Kennedy School, Belfer Center for Science and International Affairs, May 2014), p.1.

[7] Ding Ying, "A Gas Bond - Energy Cooperation Will Serve as a New Link between China and Russia," *Beijing Review*, May 22, 2014, via Factiva.

[8] Bill White, "Stakes Are Big in Russia-China Gas Supply Talks" (Alaska Natural Gas Transportation Projects: Office of the Regional Coordinator, February 11, 2013.

[9] Bill White, "Stakes Are Big in Russia-China Gas Supply Talks" (Alaska Natural Gas Transportation Projects: Office of the Regional Coordinator, February 11, 2013.

[10] Sergey Paltsev, "Scenarios for Russia's Natural Gas Exports to 2050," *Energy Economics* 42 (2014): 268; Bill White, "Stakes Are Big in Russia-China Gas Supply Talks" (Alaska Natural Gas Transportation Projects: Office of the Regional Coordinator, February 11, 2013.

[11] Keun-Wook Paik, "Through the Dragon Gate? A Window of Opportunity for Northeast Asian Gas Security" (London, UK: Chatham House, May 2012), p.12.

[12] Keun-Wook Paik, "Through the Dragon Gate? A Window of Opportunity for Northeast Asian Gas Security" (London, UK: Chatham House, May 2012), p.12.

[13] Ricki Wang, "Nationwide Gas Pricing Reform in China Raises Demand Concerns," ICIS News, July 2, 2013. *http://www.icis.com/resources/news/2013/07/02/9683579/nationwide-gas-pricing-reform-in-china-raises-demand-concerns/.*

[14] Keun-Wook Paik, "Through the Dragon Gate? A Window of Opportunity for Northeast Asian Gas Security" (London, UK: Chatham House, May 2012), p.12.

[15] Statistics from the International Energy Agency, 2012. *http://www.iea.org/publications/freepublications/publication/kwes.pdf.*

[16] Andrew Erickson and Gabriel B. Collins, "China's Oil Security Pipe Dream: The Reality, and Strategic Consequences, of Seaborne Imports," *Naval War College Review* 63:2 (Spring 2010): 90.

[17] Bill White, "Stakes Are Big in Russia-China Gas Supply Talks" (Alaska Natural Gas Transportation Projects: Office of the Regional Coordinator), February 11, 2013.

[18] Keun-Wook Paik, "The Role of Russian Gas in China's Energy Supply Strategy." *Asia Europe Journal* 11:3 (2013): 326-327.

[19] Elena Shadrina and Michael Bradshaw, "Russia's Energy Governance Transitions and Implications for Enhanced Cooperation with China, Japan, and South Korea," *Post-Soviet Affairs* 29:6 (2013): 491.

[20] Rafael Fernández and Enrique Palazuelos, "The Future of Russian Gas Exports to East Asia: Feasibility and Market Implications," *Futures* 43, no. 10 (2011): 1072.

[21] Amie Tsang, "Why Putin Needs the Gazprom Deal," *Financial Times*, May 21, 2014, via Factiva.

[22] Rafael Fernández and Enrique Palazuelos, "The Future of Russian Gas Exports to East Asia: Feasibility and Market Implications," *Futures* 43, no. 10 (2011): 1072.

[23] Elena Kropatcheva, "He Who Has the Pipeline Calls the Tune? Russia's Energy Power Against the Background of the Shale "Revolutions," *Energy Policy* 66 (2014): 5.

[24] Sergey Paltsev, "Scenarios for Russia's Natural Gas Exports to 2050," *Energy Economics* 42 (2014): 263.

[25] Elena Kropatcheva, "He Who Has the Pipeline Calls the Tune? Russia's Energy Power Against the Background of the Shale "Revolutions," *Energy Policy* 66 (2014): 3-4.

[26] Elena Kropatcheva, "He Who Has the Pipeline Calls the Tune? Russia's Energy Power Against the Background of the Shale "Revolutions," *Energy Policy* 66 (2014): 4-5.

[27] Elena Kropatcheva, "He Who Has the Pipeline Calls the Tune? Russia's Energy Power Against the Background of the Shale "Revolutions," *Energy Policy* 66 (2014): 5.

[28] Leslie Palti-Guzman, "Don't Cry for the Nabucco Pipeline," Reuters, May 1, 2014, via Factiva; Clara Weiss, "European Union's Nabucco Pipeline Project Aborted," *World Socialist Website*, July 13, 2013, via Factiva.

[29] Elena Kropatcheva, "He Who Has the Pipeline Calls the Tune? Russia's Energy Power Against the Background of the Shale "Revolutions," *Energy Policy* 66 (2014): 4-5.

[30] Rafael Fernández and Enrique Palazuelos, "The Future of Russian Gas Exports to East Asia: Feasibility and Market Implications," *Futures* 43, no. 10 (2011): 1076.

[31] Alexandros Petersen and Katinka Barysch, "Russia, China, and the Geopolitics of Energy in Central Asia," Center for European Reform (November 2011).

[32] Alexandros Petersen and Katinka Barysch, "Russia, China, and the Geopolitics of Energy in Central Asia," Center for European Reform (November 2011).

[33] RT, "Russia and China Seal Historic $400bn Gas Deal," May 21, 2014, via Factiva.

[34] Keun-Wook Paik, "The Role of Russian Gas in China's Energy Supply Strategy." *Asia Europe Journal* 11:3 (2013): 332-335.

[35] BBC, "Putin Praises Russia-China Gas Deal as Largest Ever," May 21, 2014, via Factiva.

[36] "Wood Mackenzie: Russia-China Gas Deal Opens Up 'New Europe' for Gazprom," Wood MacKenzie press release via Downstreamtoday.com, May 22, 2014. *http://www.downstreamtoday.com/News/ArticlePrint.aspx?aid=43259&AspxAutoDetectCookieSupport=1.*

[37] Rafael Fernández and Enrique Palazuelos, "The Future of Russian Gas Exports to East Asia: Feasibility and Market Implications," *Futures* 43, no. 10 (2011): 1075-1076.

[38] Keun-Wook Paik, "The Role of Russian Gas in China's Energy Supply Strategy," *Asia Europe Journal* 11:3 (2013): 334.

[39] "Wood Mackenzie: Russia-China Gas Deal Opens Up 'New Europe' for Gazprom," Wood MacKenzie press release via Downstreamtoday.com, May 22, 2014. *http://www.downstreamtoday.com/News/ArticlePrint.aspx?aid=43259&AspxAutoDetectCookieSupport=1.*

[40] Joe Parson, "China's Big Bargaining Chip Against Gazprom," *Moscow Times*, May 18, 2014.

[41] William Wan and Abigail Hauslohner, "China, Russia Sign $400 Billion Gas Deal," *Washington Post*, May 21, 2014, via Factiva.

[42] William Wan and Abigail Hauslohner, "China, Russia Sign $400 Billion Gas Deal," *Washington Post*, May 21, 2014, via Factiva.

[43] Jane Perlez, "China and Russia Reach Major Gas Deal," *New York Times*, May 21, 2014, via Factiva.

[44] Keun-Wook Paik, "The Role of Russian Gas in China's Energy Supply Strategy." *Asia Europe Journal* 11:3 (2013): 330-332.

[45] Morena Skalamera, "Booming Synergies in Sino-Russian Natural Gas Partnership," (Cambridge, MA: Harvard Kennedy School, Belfer Center for Science and International Affairs, May 2014).

[46] Jane Perlez, "China and Russia Reach Major Gas Deal," *New York Times*, May 21, 2014, via Factiva.

[47] Rafael Fernández and Enrique Palazuelos, "The Future of Russian Gas Exports to East Asia: Feasibility and Market Implications," *Futures* 43, no. 10 (2011): 1079.

[48] Sergey Paltsev, "Scenarios for Russia's Natural Gas Exports to 2050," *Energy Economics* 42 (2014): 265.

[49] RIA Novosti, "Russia-China Gas Contract Includes Take-or-Pay Provision," May 21, 2014, via Factiva.

[50] Erica Downs, "Inside China, Inc.: China Development Bank's Cross-Border Energy Deals," *Brookings John L. Thornton Monograph Series* 3, March 2011.

[51] Robert Tuttle, Anna Shiryaevskaya, and Isis Almeida, "Russia-China Deal to Damp LNG Prices as Output Rises," Bloomberg, May 22, 2014, via Factiva.

[52] Elena Shadrina and Michael Bradshaw, "Russia's Energy Governance Transitions and Implications for Enhanced Cooperation with China, Japan, and South Korea," *Post-Soviet Affairs* 29:6 (2013): 492.

[53] RIA Novosti, "Russian Finance Ministry to Consider Tax Breaks on Gas Deliveries to China," May 22, 2014, via Factiva.

[54] Joe Parson, "China's Big Bargaining Chip Against Gazprom," *The Moscow Times*, May 18, 2014.

[55] Michael Birnbaum, "Russia Threatens Embattled Ukraine with Cutoff of Gas," *Washington Post*, June 1, 2014, via Factiva.

[56] CCTV-Xinwen, "Sino-Russian 'Joint Sea-2014' Exercise Features 'Three First Times,'" Television, May 20, 2014. Hosted by Open Source Center. ID: CHR2014052031570550.

[57] Peter Dunai and Matthew Smith, "Russia, China S-400 Deal Moves Forward," March 31, 2014. *http://www.janes.com/article/36226/russia-china-s-400-deal-moves-forward*; *Want China Times* (Taiwan), "Russia to Give China More Advanced Submarine Technology," March 25, 2014. *http://www.wantchinatimes.com/news-subclass-cnt.aspx?cid=1101&MainCatID=11&id=20140325000079*; Peter Wood, "How China Plans to Use the Su-35," *Diplomat*, November 27, 2013. *http://thediplomat.com/2013/11/how-china-plans-to-use-the-su-35/?allpages=yes;* BBC News, "China 'Buys Fighter Jets and Submarines from Russia,'" March 25, 2013. *http://www.bbc.co.uk/news/world-asia-21930280.*

[58] *Beijing Youth Daily* (Beijing Qingnian Bao), "Xi Jinping Meets Putin: Cannot Allow Tragedy of Militarist Invasions to Be Repeated [Xi Jinping huiwu Pujing: juebu xu junguo zhuyi qinlue beiju chongyan]," May 21, 2014.

[59] Swaran Singh, "Xi's Proactive Foreign Policy Fruitful," *China Daily*, March 19, 2014. *http://www.chinadaily.com.cn/opinion/2014-03/19/content_17358201.htm*; Leslie Gelb and Dimitri Simes, "A New Anti-American Axis?" *New York Times*, July 6, 2013. *http://www.nytimes.com/2013/07/07/opinion/sunday/a-new-anti-americanaxis.html?pagewanted=all&_r=0.*

[60] Yu Bin, "China-Russia Relations: 'Western Civil War' Déjà Vu?" *Comparative Connections* 15:3 (May 2014). *http://csis.org/publication/comparative-connections-v16-n1-china-russia.*

[61] Michelle Nichols and Louis Charbonneau, "Russia, China Veto U.N. Bid to Refer Syria to International Court," Reuters, May 23, 2014. *http://www.reuters.com/article/2014/05/23/us-syria-crisis-un-icc-idUSBREA4M03220140523.*

[62] RIA Novosti, "Russia, China to Closely Coordinate Actions in UN Security Council," May 14, 2014, via Factiva.

[63] Lu Yu, "Commentary: West Should Work With, not Against, Russia in Handling Ukraine Crisis," *Xinhua* (English edition), March 3, 2014. *http://news.xinhuanet.com/english/indepth/2014-03/03/c_133154966.htm.*

[64] Deutsche Welle, "Moscow Aims to Trade Energy for Chinese Investment in Russia," May 21, 2014 via Factiva.

[65] Angus Grigg, "China's Xi Warns US to Stay Out of Asia," *The Australian Financial Review*, May 22, 2014, via Factiva.

[66] Steve Gutterman, "Putin Tells Investors Russia Wants Good Ties, Respect," Reuters, May 22, 2014, via Factiva; *Beijing Youth Daily* (Beijing Qingnian Bao), "Xi Jinping Meets Putin: Cannot Allow Tragedy of Militarist Invasions to Be Repeated [Xi Jinping huiwu Pujing: juebu xu junguo zhuyi qinlue beiju chongyan]," May 21, 2014.

[67] Alexandros Petersen and Katinka Barysch, "Russia, China, and the Geopolitics of Energy in Central Asia," Center for European Reform (November 2011).

[68] Andrew C. Kuchins, "Russia and CIS in 2013: Russia's Pivot to Asia," *Asian Survey* 54:1 (January/February 2014): 136.

[69] Andrew C. Kuchins, "Russia and CIS in 2013: Russia's Pivot to Asia," *Asian Survey* 54:1 (January/February 2014): 135.

[70] Alexandros Petersen and Katinka Barysch, "Russia, China, and the Geopolitics of Energy in Central Asia," Center for European Reform (November 2011).

[71] Morena Skalamera, "Booming Synergies in Sino-Russian Natural Gas Partnership" (Cambridge, MA: Harvard Kennedy School, Belfer Center for Science and International Affairs, May 2014).

[72] Morena Skalamera, "Booming Synergies in Sino-Russian Natural Gas Partnership" (Cambridge, MA: Harvard Kennedy School, Belfer Center for Science and International Affairs, May 2014).

[73] RIA Novosti, "Outcomes of Putin's Visit to China, Multiple Achievements of Day One," May 20, 2014, via Factiva.

[74] Denis Pinchuk and Lidia Kelly, "Gazprom Unit, Novatek Sign Deal on Yamal Gas Supply," May 23, 2014, via Factiva.

[75] Morena Skalamera, "Booming Synergies in Sino-Russian Natural Gas Partnership" (Cambridge, MA: Harvard Kennedy School, Belfer Center for Science and International Affairs, May 2014); RIA Novosti, "Rosneft Expects Increase in Gas Production of up to 30Bln Cubic Meters," May 22, 2014, via Factiva.

[76] *Twenty-First Century Business Herald*, "China and Russia Sign over 30 Cooperation Agreements [Zhong'e qianshu 30 duo fen hezuo xieyi]," May 21, 2014, via Factiva.

[77] RIA Novosti, "Outcomes of Putin's Visit to China, Multiple Achievements of Day One," May 20, 2014, via Factiva.

[78] Xinhua, "China and Russia to Jointly Construct Refinery in Tianjin with 16 Million Ton Capacity [Zhong'e lianhe jian Tianjin lianyouchang nian channeng jiang da 1600 wan dun]," May 22, 2014, via Factiva.

[79] Katya Golubkova, "Russia Targets Shale Oil Boom by Next Decade," Reuters, May 22, 2014, via Factiva.

[80] Reuters, "Putin Ally Expects Flurry of China Deals in New Role," May 22, 2014, via Factiva.

[81] Ding Ying, "A Gas Bond - Energy Cooperation Will Serve as a New Link between China and Russia," *Beijing Review*, May 22, 2014, via Factiva.

[82] Wall Street CN, "Progress on Abandoning the Dollar: China and Russia Increase Currency Swaps [Qu meiyuanhua jinxing shi: Zhong'e jiada zhijie huobi jiaoyi]," May 21, 2014, via Factiva; RT, "Russia's VTB and Bank of China Agree on Domestic Currency Settlements," May 20, 2014. *http://rt.com/business/160124-vtb-bank-china-currencies/ http://rt.com/business/160124-vtb-bank-china-currencies/.*

[83] *The BRICS Post*, "China-Russia Discussing Currency Swaps Package," May 9, 2014. *http://thebricspost.com/china-russia-discussing-currency-swaps-package/#.U4TisPldXmc.*

[84] RIA Novosti, "Outcomes of Putin's Visit to China, Multiple Achievements of Day One," May 20, 2014, via Factiva.

[85] Raffaello Pantucci and Alexandros Petersen, "China's Inadvertent Empire," *The National Interest* (November-December 2012).

[86] Prime News, "Russian Grids Signs Cooperation Deal with Chinese Grid Firm," May 20, 2014, via Factiva.

[87] Li Xuejing, "[Jilin yu E Suma Jituan ni hejian Zalubinuo wanneng haigang]," Xinhua, May 23, 2014, via Factiva.

[88] Huanqiu Net, "Russian Media: China and Russia Could Jointly Develop Large Aircraft; Russia May Transfer Aerospace Technology to China [E'mei: Zhong'e jiang heyan da feiji, E huo duihua kaifang hangkong jishu]," May 21, 2014, via Factiva.

[89] *Twenty-First Century Business Herald*, "China and Russia Sign over 30 Cooperation Agreements [Zhong'e qianshu 30 duo fen hezuo xieyi]," May 21, 2014, via Factiva.

[90] RIA Novosti, "Outcomes of Putin's Visit to China, Multiple Achievements of Day One," May 20, 2014, via Factiva.

[91] Ria Novosti, "Russia's Gazprom Plans First Direct Gas Deliveries to China in 2019," May 23, 2014, via Factiva.

[92] *The BRICS Post*, "China-Russia Discussing Currency Swaps Package," May 9, 2014. *http://thebricspost.com/china-russia-discussing-currency-swaps-package/#.U4TisPldXmc*.

[93] Ria Novosti, "SPIEF to Unite Businesses Worldwide Amid Looming Sanctions and Contraction," May 21, 2014, via Factiva.

[94] *The Economist*, "Economic and Financial Indicators," May 3, 2014, p.80

[95] Deutsche Welle, "Moscow Aims to Trade Energy for Chinese Investment in Russia," May 21, 2014 via Factiva.

[96] *The BRICS Post*, "China-Russia Discussing Currency Swaps Package," May 9, 2014. *http://thebricspost.com/china-russia-discussing-currency-swaps-package/#.U4TisPldXmc*.

[97] Robert Tuttle, Anna Shiryaevskaya, and Isis Almeida, "Russia-China Deal to Damp LNG Prices as Output Rises," Bloomberg, May 22, 2014, via Factiva.

[98] Robert Tuttle, Anna Shiryaevskaya, and Isis Almeida, "Russia-China Deal to Damp LNG Prices as Output Rises," Bloomberg, May 22, 2014, via Factiva.

[99] Xinhua, "China Gas Deal Not to Affect EU Supplies: IEA," May 22, 2014, via Factiva.

[100] Rafael Fernández and Enrique Palazuelos, "The Future of Russian Gas Exports to East Asia: Feasibility and Market Implications," *Futures* 43, no. 10 (2011): 1079.

[101] Mari Iwata, "Japan Looks to Stay on Tap for Russian Energy," *Wall Street Journal*, May 21, 2014, via Factiva.

[102] Rafael Fernández and Enrique Palazuelos, "The Future of Russian Gas Exports to East Asia: Feasibility and Market Implications," *Futures* 43, no. 10 (2011): 1075.

[103] Mari Iwata, "Japan Looks to Stay on Tap for Russian Energy," *Wall Street Journal*, May 21, 2014, via Factiva.

[104] "Kerry Says Russia-China Gas Deal Not Linked to Ukraine," Reuters, May 21, 2014, via Factiva.

[105] Spencer Ackerman, "Ukraine Crisis: U.S. Senators 'Frustrated' with White House Sanctions Strategy," *The Guardian*, May 6, 2014. *http://www.theguardian.com/world/2014/may/06/us-senators-white-house-russia-sanctions-ukraine*.

[106] Ian Traynor, "Obama and Merkel Warn of Tougher Sanctions against Russia over Ukraine," *The Guardian*, June 4, 2014. *http://www.theguardian.com/world/2014/jun/04/obama-russia-dark-tactics-ukraine*.

[107] RIA Novosti, "Russia-China Cooperation to Motivate EU to Strengthen Ties With Moscow – Foreign Ministry," May 23, 2014, via Factiva.

[108] Louise Watt and Vladimir Isachenkov, "China Signs 30-Year Deal for Russian Natural Gas," Associated Press, May 21, 2014, via Factiva.

[109] Michael Birnbaum, "Russia Threatens Embattled Ukraine with Cutoff of Gas," *Washington Post*, June 1, 2014, via Factiva.